always on my mind 3

the best is yet to come 10

call me irresponsible 15

can't buy me love 22

can't help falling in love 46

come fly with me 30

comin' home baby 36

everything 51

feeling good 58

home 66

the best of
michael bublé

AF074152

how can you mend a broken heart 72

I'm your man 75

lost 86

save the last dance for me 91

a song for you 98

sway (quien sera) 105

that's life 108

try a little tenderness 116

the way you look tonight 121

you don't know me 124

Published by
Hal Leonard

Exclusive distributors:

Hal Leonard
7777 West Bluemound Road,
Milwaukee, WI 53213
Email: info@halleonard.com

Hal Leonard Europe Limited
42 Wigmore Street Marylebone,
London, WIU 2 RN
Email: info@halleonardeurope.com

Hal Leonard Australia Pty. Ltd.
4 Lentara Court Cheltenham,
Victoria, 9132 Australia
Email: info@halleonard.com.au

Order No. AM996545
ISBN 978-1-84772-936-1
This book is © Dopyright 2009 by Hal Leonard

Compiled by Nick Crispin.
Cover Design by Michael Bell Design.
Music edited by Jenni Wheeler.

For all works contained herein:
Unauthorized copying, arranging, adapting,
recording, Internet posting, public performance, or
other distribution of the music in this publication is an
infringement of copyright.
Infringers are liable under the law.

Printed in EU.

www.halleonard.com

Always On My Mind

Words & Music by Mark James, Wayne Thompson & Johnny Christopher

© Copyright 1971 (Renewed 1979) Sebanine Music Incorporated/Budde Songs Incorporated, USA.
Screen Gems-EMI Music Limited (75%)/Chelsea Music Publishing Company Limited (25%).
All Rights Reserved. International Copyright Secured.

Call Me Irresponsible

Words by Sammy Cahn
Music by Jimmy Van Heusen

*Recorded a half step higher.

© Copyright 1963 Paramount Music Corporation/Famous Music Corporation, USA.
All Rights Reserved. International Copyright Secured.

Can't Buy Me Love

Words & Music by John Lennon & Paul McCartney

Come Fly With Me

Words by Sammy Cahn
Music by Jimmy Van Heusen

© Copyright 1958 Maraville Music Corporation, USA/Cahn Music Company, USA.
Chelsea Music Publishing Company Limited (50%)/Warner/Chappell North America Limited (50%).
All Rights Reserved. International Copyright Secured.

Comin' Home Baby

Words by Bob Dorough
Music by Ben Tucker

Can't Help Falling In Love

Words & Music by George David Weiss, Hugo Peretti & Luigi Creatore

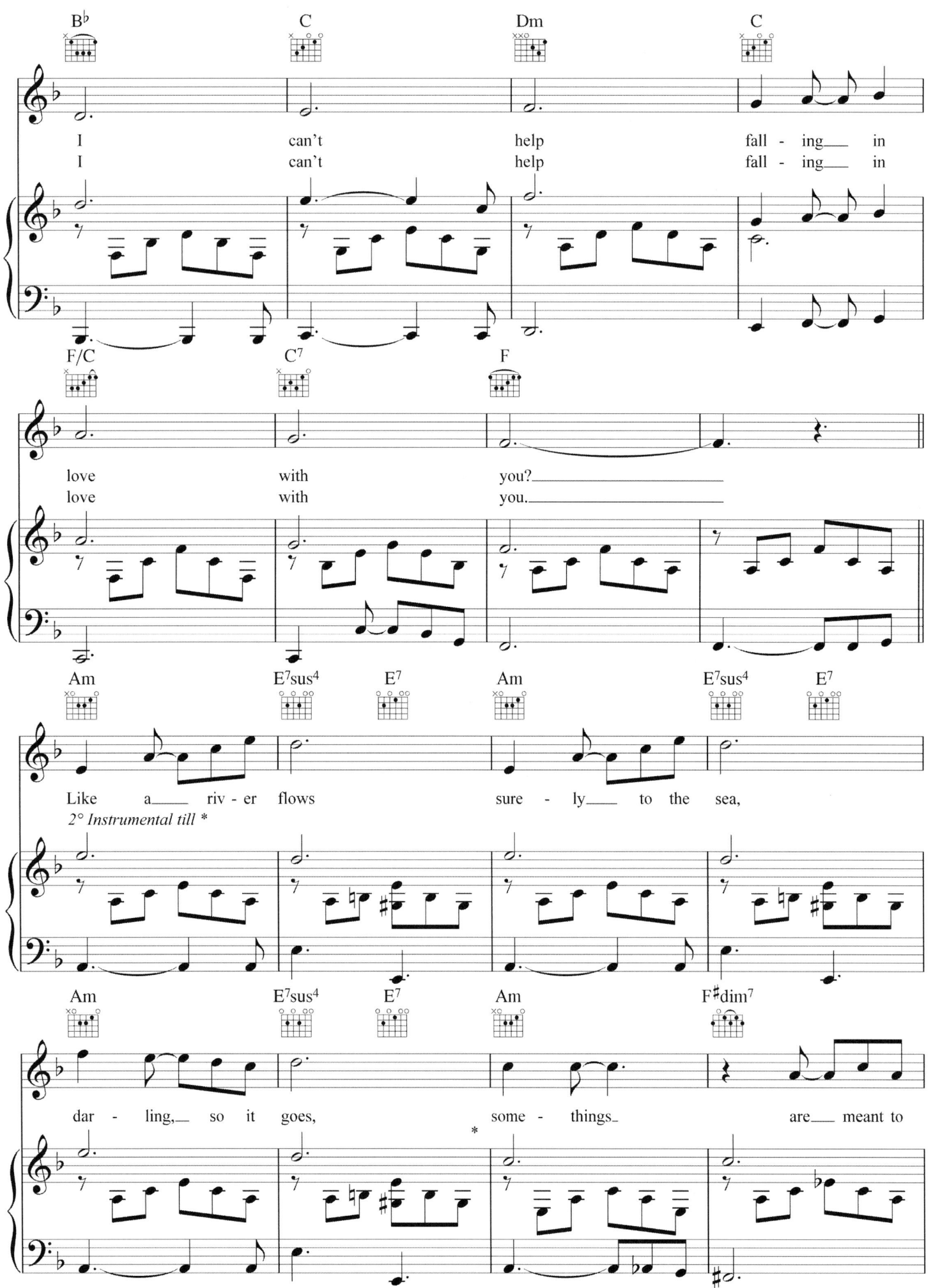

Everything

Words & Music by Michael Bublé, Alan Chang & Gillies Foster

Feeling Good

Words & Music by Leslie Bricusse & Anthony Newley

Home

Words & Music by Michael Bublé, Alan Chang & Amy Foster Gilles

How Can You Mend A Broken Heart

Words & Music by Barry Gibb & Robin Gibb

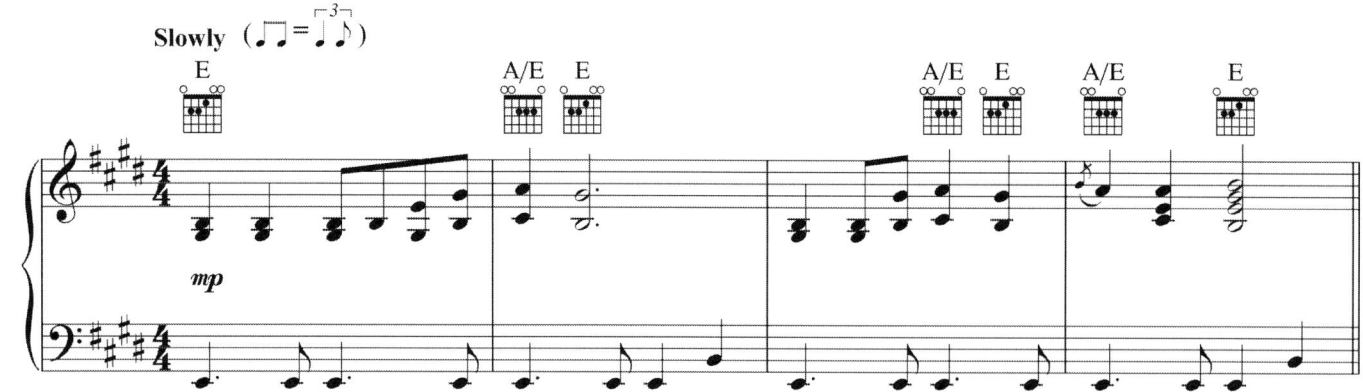

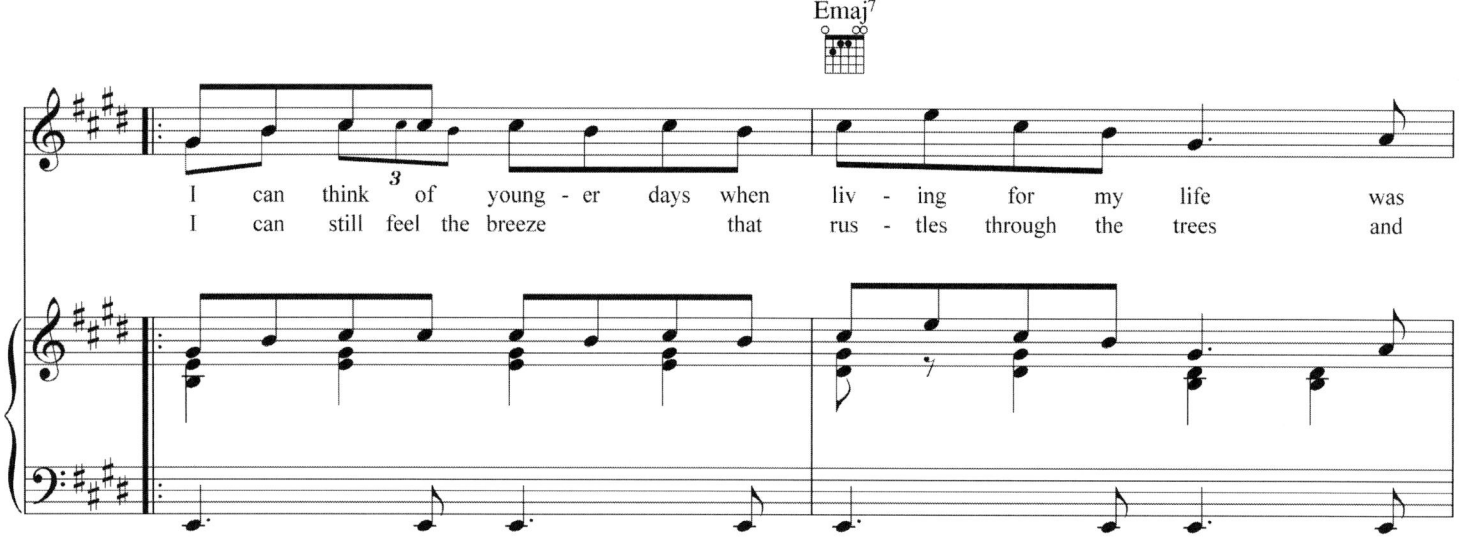

I can think of young-er days when liv-ing for my life was
I can still feel the breeze that rus-tles through the trees and

ev-'ry-thing a man could want to do. I could nev-er see to-
mist-y mem-o-ries of days gone by. We could nev-er see to-

© Copyright 1971 Crompton Songs (50%)/Gibb Brothers Music (50%).
Warner/Chappell Music Limited (50%)/Universal Music Publishing MGB Limited (50%).
All Rights Reserved. International Copyright Secured.

I'm Your Man

Words & Music by Leonard Cohen

*Recorded a half step lower.

© Copyright 1988 Sony/ATV Music Publishing (UK) Limited.
All Rights Reserved. International Copyright Secured.

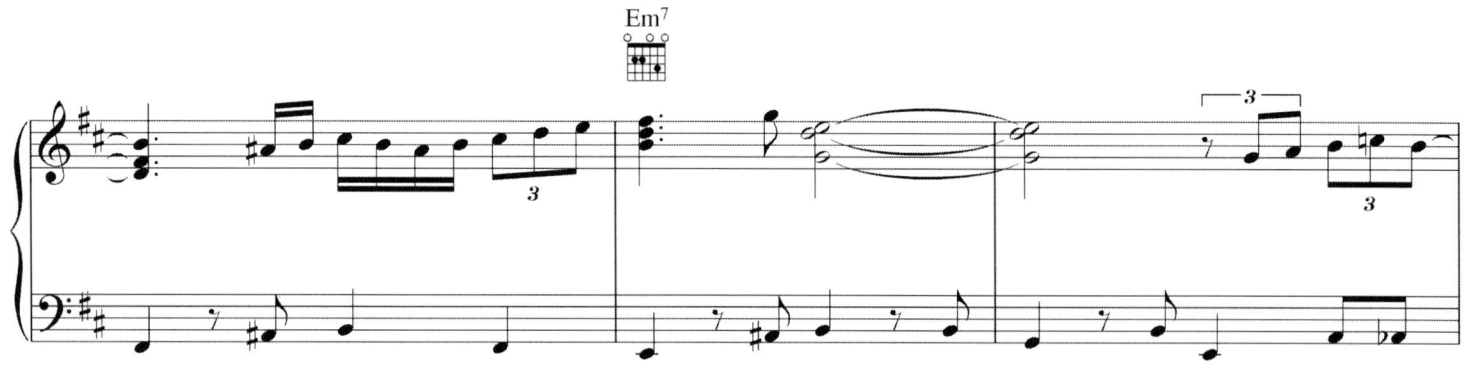

Lost

Words & Music by Michael Bublé, Alan Chang & Jann Richards

Original key B major

Save The Last Dance For Me

Words & Music by Doc Pomus & Mort Shuman

A Song For You
Words & Music by Leon Russell

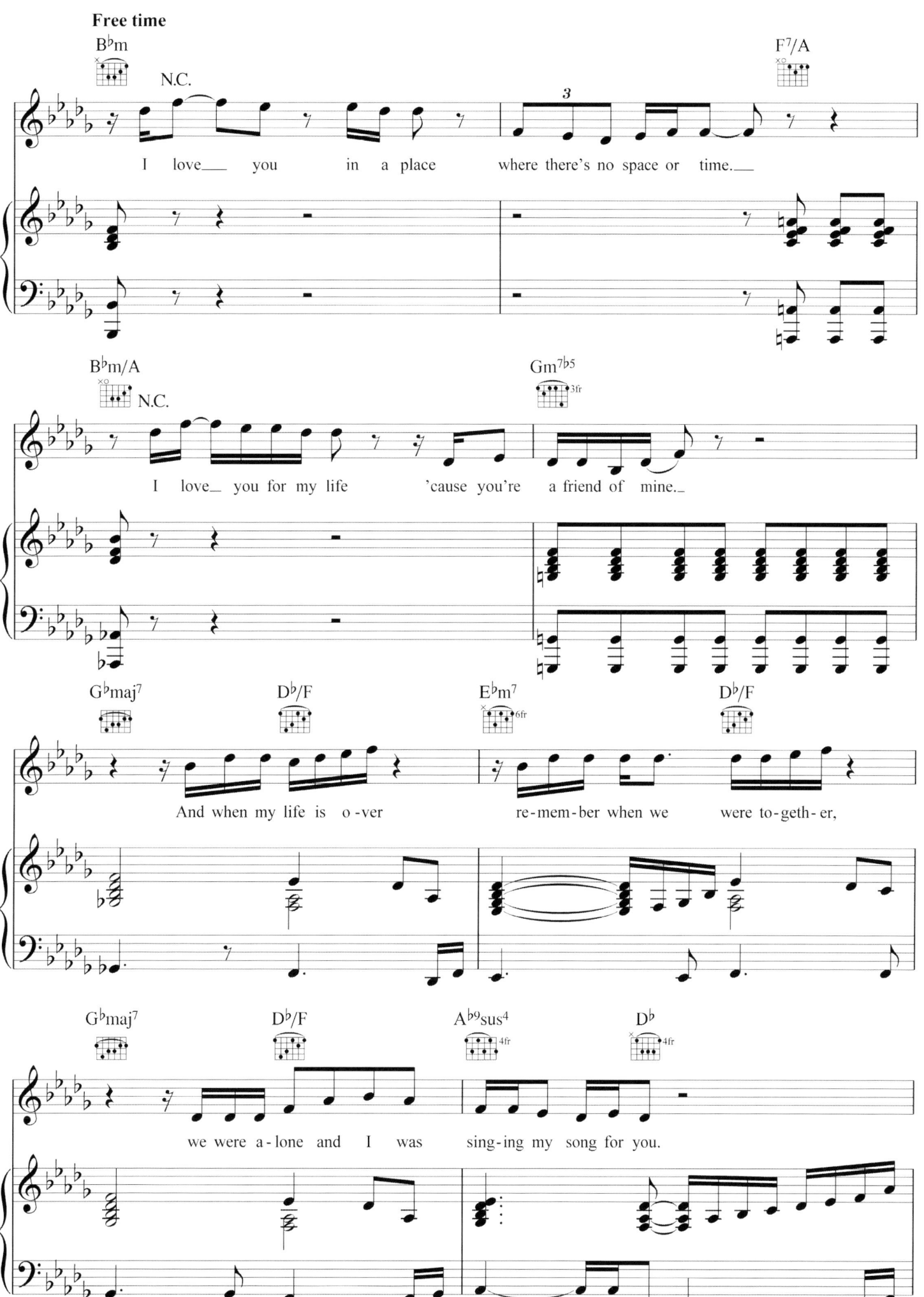

That's Life

Words & Music by Dean Kay & Kelly Gordon

© Copyright 1964 Universal Music Publishing Limited
All rights in Germany administered by Universal Music Publ. GmbH.
All Rights Reserved. International Copyright Secured.

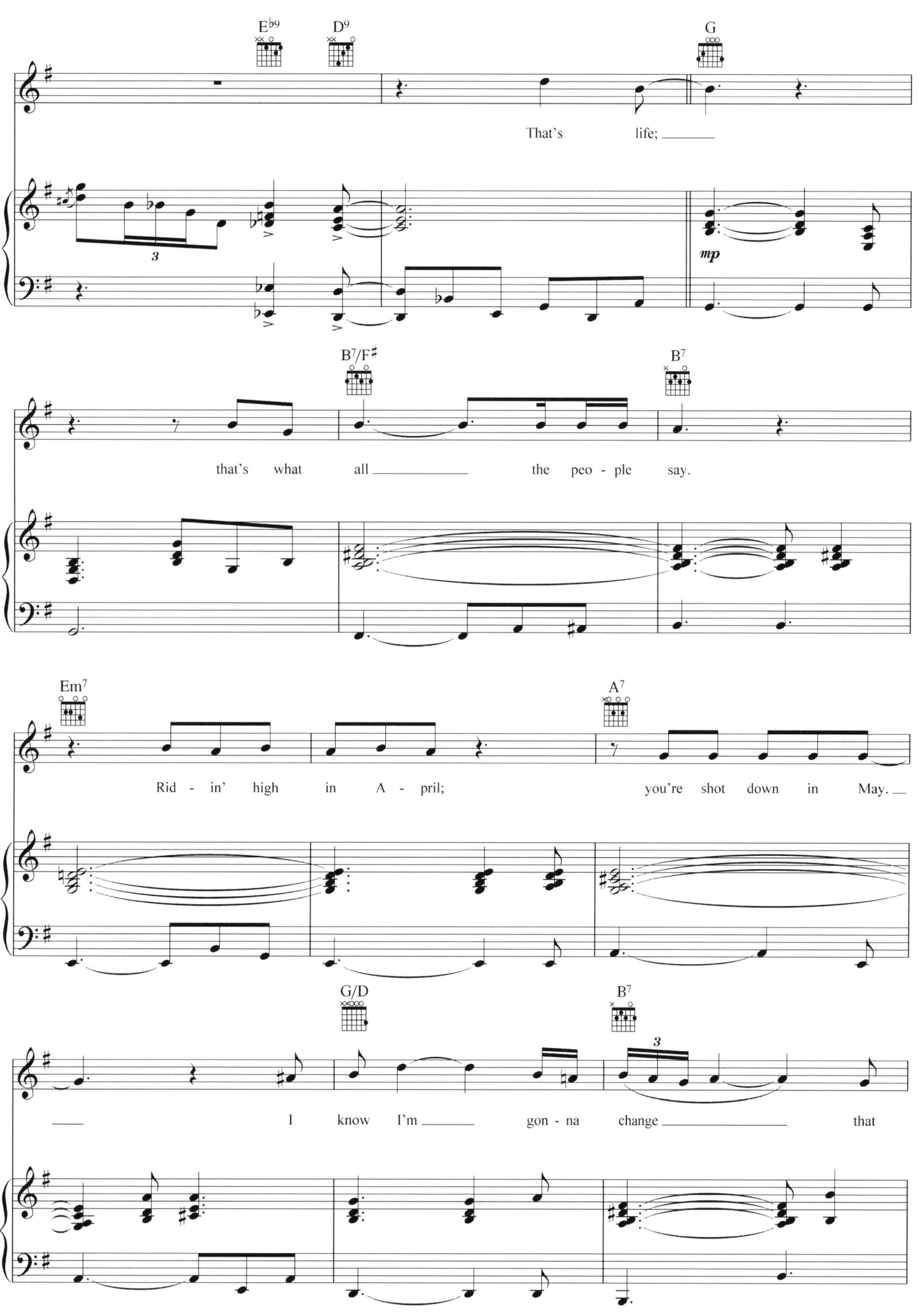

The Way You Look Tonight

Words by Dorothy Fields
Music by Jerome Kern

© Copyright 1936 T.B. Harms & Company Incorporated, USA.
Shapiro Bernstein & Company Limited (50%)/Universal Music Publishing Limited (50%) (administered in Germany by Universal Music Publ. GmbH).
All Rights Reserved. International Copyright Secured.

You Don't Know Me

Words & Music by Cindy Walker & Eddy Arnold